P9-CIT-182

Portugal

4th edition. Text and photographs updated

Portugal

by **Carlos Vitorino da Silva Barros**

PUBLISHED BY CENTRO DE TURISMO
DA RODOVIÁRIA NACIONAL E. P.   LISBON

© Copyright by Carlos Vitorino da Silva Barros — 1978
Printed in Portugal by Artistas Reunidos — Porto

SUBJECT INDEX OF PLATES

PORTUGAL "Garden of Europe, planted by the sea..."

FROM THE FOUNDATION TILL 1640

According to several historians, and positive evidence, it seems that the strip of land that stretches alongside the Ocean on the western coast of the Iberian Peninsula—which is at present Portugal—has been inhabited from very early times.

By Ligurians? By Celts? Or by the latter, with the Iberians, merged in the so-called Celt-Iberians? Such are the current hypotheses, in view of the evidence pointing towards the existence of ancient local civilizations.

Much later came the Phoenicians—great and far-travelling merchants—who established trading posts along the coast of the Peninsula. The Greeks arrived after the 7th Century B.C., followed somewhat later by the Carthaginians, who stayed on until the wars with the famous legions of Rome.

And it is at this stage that the first mention of the Lusitanians appears (*circa* 150 B.C.).

Leaders such as Viriato stand in History as forerunners. almost demi-gods, embodying the spirit of independence that was doomed to be conquered.

Can the Lusitanians be truly considered as ancestors of the Portuguese? After having read the opinion of the historians, one is, at any rate, ready to accept a certain identity of characteristics between the two peoples.

Rome achieved the conquest of the Peninsula, but the latter was not the loser; on the contrary, like the rest of Western Europe, it developed considerably.

By the beginning of the 5th Century A.D., the Barbarian invasions became increasingly menacing and Rome, already decadent, could not resist the invaders.

For over one hundred years the Swabians held a large territory north of the Tagus with Braga as their capital, and this territory soon took the name of Portu-Cale. A little later on came the Visigoths, who joined the Swabians in conversion to the Christian Faith. Peace, however, was not to last very long.

In 711 the Arabs, who had been dreaming of conquering the Iberian Peninsula, crossed the straits of Gibraltar and invaded Southern Spain.

Eight years later the whole of the Peninsula had been occupied. And for eight centuries they remained. It was only in 1492, with the conquest of the Kingdom of Granada by the Catholic Monarchs Ferdinand and Isabella, that the Arab rule ultimately came to an end.

But let us turn to the eleventh century. By then, Christian Kingdoms had thrown back the invaders from the northern mountainous areas, but these communities were constantly in deadly peril. Time went by, and Alphonso, King of Leon, appealed to France for volunteers.

Under the inspiration of Cluny—the great Benedictine centre—a group of French Knights, including Henri Count of Burgundy and his cousin Raymond, came and joined Alphonso VI. The latter, aged and foreseeing future difficulties, married his eldest daughter,

Urraca, to Raymond, and Teresa to Henri. To the former was given the government of the country of Galicia and of the land lying between the Minho and Douro rivers; to the latter was given, at a slightly later date, the government of the territory between the Minho and Tagus rivers, with the capital at Coimbra.

By 1097 Henri already described himself as "Count of Portucale". Quarrels and fighting followed, before the independence of Portugal could become a fact. Negotiations and treaties were clearly means of temporary compromise.

Henri died and his widow, Teresa, began to be influenced by interests other than the construction of the future State, thus causing general displeasure. Only a few years later, in 1128, a bitter battle was fought not far from Guimarães, between the son and heir of Teresa, young Afonso Henriques, and his cousin the young ruler of Galicia.

The ensuing victory may be considered as the foundation stone of the Portuguese Nation.

The Arab threat, however, was always present.

In 1147, helped by Crusaders from Northern Europe, who were on their way to the Holy Land, he conquered Santarém, Lisbon, Sintra, and several other Moorish strongholds.

In order to increase the defensive power of the newly-formed kingdom, he granted many privileges to the Military and Religious Orders.

The Templars, who had come to Portugal as early as 1128, made their headquarters at the Castle of Tomar in 1160.

With the foundation of the Monastery of Alcobaça the part to be played by the Cistercians in Portuguese History began, and the consequences were political (influence of St. Bernard in Rome), cultural (foundation of schools), and social (definition of rights concerning property, assistance, etc.), all of them of great moment.

The full task of the conquest of the territory and strengthening of independence was completed under King Afonso III, with the definitive control of the Algarve (the southernmost province) from 1249.

The country developed in many ways, namely in the political, the social and the economic spheres.

King Denis was remarkable, for his or any time. He was keenly interested in study and created the University, at first in Lisbon, then transferred to Coimbra in 1308. He was also a wise protector of agriculture and ordered the plantation of the Leiria pine forest, partly to avoid the inland progress of the dunes, along the coast.

He showed his particular foresight and intelligence at the time when the Order of the Templars was extinguished.

While Philippe le Bel, in France, endeavoured to stifle and destroy the Order, the King of Portugal, in the best interests of the cause of his God and his Country, converted the now discredited Order into the Order of Christ (1319).

His wife, Queen Isabel of Aragon (a niece of Elizabeth of Hungary), whose outstanding virtue is recorded in many a touching episode, merited the honour of canonization.

Afonso IV was the successor of Denis. It was towards the end of his reign that the famous love episode of Inês de Castro took place. The tragic story of the lovers, Inês and Pedro, the King's own son, rendered immortal by many poets, has lost its historical proportions to become a beautiful legend.

Prince Pedro's marriage to Constança of Castille had been arranged, for political reasons, in 1336. Among the ladies in attendance on the bride was Inês de Castro, whose exceptional beauty enthralled Pedro.

Serious problems soon arose in the private life of the couple, and Princess Constança died after their third child was born.

The danger of Inês exerting influence over Pedro seemed to several people a serious one, all the more as her brothers were generally disliked by the Portuguese people, on account of their scheming for their own ends.

They tried to persuade the Prince to claim the Crown of Castille, profiting from the rather involved situation following the death of Alfonso XI.

And so it came about that what would otherwise have been a private love affair became a matter of state. Afonso IV of Portugal himself feared that under the influence of Inês his son might start on such a venture.

The interest of the State prevailed, and Inês was executed in Coimbra, by royal decision, and for the good of the realm, as it was thought.

Inês and Pedro, who according to Pedro's later declaration had been secretly married, now rest in beautiful twin Gothic tombs in the Monastery of Alcobaça.

In 1367 Fernando ascended the throne. Young, ambitious and adventurous, he placed the country in more than one embarrassing situation.

His great ambition led him in the end to the signing of a treaty with Castille in dishonourable circumstances. Meanwhile, having become aware of Edward III of England's intentions concerning the throne of Castille, he signed an Alliance with the latter, in 1373, by which, in turn, England undertook to defend Portugal's rights.

On the death of Fernando the Crown should have passed to his daughter Beatriz, who was married to the king of Castille. This created a new and vital problem and was the cause of more wars and fighting between the two Peninsular States, Portugal and Castille.

King Fernando's widow remained as Regent for some time, but discontent increased among the people. The validity of the succession was questioned; the people, growing more and more impatient, elected João, who was Master of the Order of Avis, to be Defender of the Realm, and he was soon joined by another young man, Nuno Álvares Pereira.

The "Cortes" (Parliament) were held in Coimbra some time later and João of Avis was elected King, thus becoming João I. The King of Castille would not, obviously, accept this decision, and the resulting battle was fought at Aljubarrota (approximately halfway between Alcobaça and Batalha), on August 14th, 1385, and was a decisive victory for Portugal. The living testimony of this day of glory for the colours of Portugal is the majestic Monastery of Batalha, built in fulfilment of a vow made by the new King before the battle began.

Several of the blood connections between the Royal Houses of Portugal and of other countries date from this period, namely the marriage of Princess Isabel, daughter of João I and of his wife Philippa of Lancaster, to Philippe le Bon, Duke of Burgundy.

A new era began with João I, which took the form of the rise of Portugal beyond the seas (eventually from Newfoundland in the west, to the coast of Australia, in the east).

The first voyage that definitely marks the beginning of this period is the expedition to, and conquest of, Ceuta, in North Africa, in 1415, led by the King himself, with his sons Duarte, Pedro and Henrique, who were knighted in the field.

And so began one of the greatest epics in the History of Mankind as the navigators of Portugal sailed further from their home, and for two centuries carried inseparably together to the farthest corners of the Earth, the Cross of Christ and the Flag of Portugal.

Prince Henry—the Navigator—was the mind and heart of this enterprise, truly a Crusade, as confirmed by the Bull of Pope Nicholas V in 1455.

After he returned from Ceuta, Prince Henrique gave his whole undivided attention to the cause of the sea. At the southern end of Portugal, at Sagres, he created the centre of research and study for which he summoned, invited and hired the greatest geographers and mathematicians of his time, to examine—and eventually to solve—the fundamental problems of open sea navigation. New types of ship were built, the *Caravela* and the *Nau*—better suited to the long voyages on the terrifying unknown seas.

The legend of the invincible sea was destroyed for ever.

And the most daring plan that 15th Century man could conceive was gradually prepared and carried out: the discovery of the sea route to India. The Prince at Sagres—hence called the Prince of Sagres—went on looking out towards the sea, discovering and unveilling its mysteries. New lands were found along the coast of Africa, and some in the Atlantic also, such as Madeira, Azores, Cape Verde, etc.

The Prince's father, his brothers Duarte and Pedro and Fernando, had died in the meantime. After his own death in 1460, the work was carried on especially by João II, a king who is not only a symbol of absolute monarchy, but also the far-seeing mind that gave the fullest impulse and direction to Portuguese maritime expansion in the 15th Century.

But the programme of discovery as outlined under Prince Henrique was ever present.

Bartolomeu Dias sailed to the very south of the African continent and the name of Cape of Storms was changed to Cape of Good Hope.

About 1481, Christopher Colombus, already married to a Portuguese, the daughter of navigator Bartolomeu Perestrelo, offered his services for new discoveries. The King, however, was not greatly impressed by the plan—and notice what a strange character this man Colombus presents, veiled in mystery, not letting us know for certain his nationality even: Genoese? Spanish? Portuguese? The final answer will probably remain forever unregistered in the annals of History.

Once his services had been refused by the King of Portugal, Colombus turned to the sovereigns of Spain, and aided especially by Isabella "the Catholic", he finally got his commission and sailed towards what would be the discovery of the American Continent, in 1492.

Years went by. Manuel I—the Fortunate King—now wore the Crown of Portugal. The dream of the route to India was finally coming true. On the 8th of July, 1497 a small fleet of four ships commanded by Vasco da Gama sailed from the Tagus.

1498—the month of May. After ten months of sacrifice, struggle, dauntless faith, the Portuguese ships reached Calicut, in India.

A gigantic achievement indeed, to be for ever remembered as long as men have memories.

King Manuel continued earlier plans, and in 1500 a fleet commanded by Pedro Álvares Cabral reached the shores of Brazil. According to some historians, however, this "discovery" was rather in the nature of a political act, assuming that the Portuguese already knew of the existence of land in those parts.

Another remarkable Portuguese navigator appeared at this time, Magalhães — or Magellan — who sailed round the World commissioned by Spain. Althoug an enterprise of the Spanish State, the voyage was to a very great extent prepared by Portuguese experts.

The Portuguese Empire was, in the meantime, growing to gigantic proportions. It is not possible in this very brief summary to refer to the many consequences of the Portuguese Discoveries. Let us point out, however, that the opening of the route to India threatened Arab supremacy over the Red Sea, while the Turkish Empire of Constantinople lost all possibilities of expanding, and Venice yielded to Lisbon its key position as emporium for Eastern goods.

Lisbon thus became perhaps the most flourishing town in the world, and the Tagus was for a time the very centre of European trade.

The sciences also, such as geography, cartography, medicine etc., as well as architecture and the arts, were deeply influenced as a result of the Discoveries.

To commemorate the great deeds of the Portuguese, King Manuel ordered the construction, beginning about 1500, of the Monastery of Jerónimos, close to the beach from which the Portuguese caravels had sailed, leaving behind them many a sad farewell filled with uncertainty.

The motifs of the sea — ropes, seaweed, caravels, shells — the fauna and flora of the newly discovered areas and continents, particularly of India, were the sources of inspiration of our artists ("Manueline" style).

It can be said without hesitation that the Monastery of Jerónimos, the *Lusíadas* — the epic by our greatest poet, Camões (16th century) — and the poliptych attributed to the painter Nuno Gonçalves, stand as imperishable symbols which will forever evoke the glory of Portugal.

João III, succeeded Manuel in 1521.

The problems arising out of Portugal's greatness were many and vast. Envy, and disrespect for conventions, among other things, soon caused very serious troubles and irreparable losses.

At this time all Europe was being reached by the fires of the Reformation, which the German monk Martin Luther had started. João III, desirous of serving the cause of God, like his ancestors, asked the Pope for permission to establish the Inquisition. At about the same time there came to Portugal the first members of the Jesuit Order, probably the Reformation's most bitter adversary, which had recently been founded in Spain by Saint Ignatius of Loyola.

In golden pages of the History of Portuguese Civilization there will always be read the names of several Jesuit missionaries: Saint Francis Xavier, Apostle of India; José de Anchieta and Manuel da Nóbrega, missionaries in Brazil.

With the death of João III, the Crown passed to young Sebastião, who was only 14 years old. He felt in his veins the old undaunted courage of his race, but insufficiently seasoned, perhaps, due to the unripeness of his years. His dream and goal was North Africa, which he would like to make an advanced post of Portugal. A gigantic expedition was prepared and over 500 ships finally sailed carrying the flower of the country's youth. The battle was fought at Alcacer-Quibir in 1578. The date is a tragic one in our History, for in that battle were lost not only the life of the brave young "God's Captain", as was his ardent desire, but with him also the great majority of the young nobility of Portugal.

The star of Portugal began to fail. Cardinal Henrique, an old man, succeeded. The people began to fear the increasing claims of Philip II of Spain, who was a grandson of Manuel I of Portugal, by the latter's eldest daughter Isabel. There were other claimants to the throne, the most popular of whom was António "Prior" of Crato, son of the late Prince Luís.

António was eventually chosen by the people. Philip II, however, did not accept the solution and sent the Duke of Alba with a powerful army, who defeated António and forced him into exile.

The "Cortes" summoned at Tomar in 1580 established a Dualistic monarchy. Philip II more or less respected his promise that Portuguese integrity would be unhinderèd. His successors, Philip III and Philip IV, however, did not, and discontent grew rapidly, all the more as the country was receiving heavy blows, particularly the loss of practically the entire navy in 1588 in the war between Spain and England (the Invincible Armada).

It was a period of humiliation for Portugal, but liberation appeared for a time impossible. Deep in their hearts the Portuguese kept hoping for the return of King Sebastião, since the young "God's Captain" had not been found among the dead on the field at Alcácer-Quibir. "Sebastianism" was the opiate found to cherish the hope of the Portuguese in this time of sadness.

Meanwhile, France and the House of Austria, which was also the reigning House in Spain, were fighting each other, and Louis XIII of France sent his envoys to Portugal. The oppression, very strict under Philip IV, could no longer be tolerated.

On the morning of the 1st of December, 1640, a group of patriots approached the Palace where the Deputies of the Spanish King, the Duchess of Mantua and the traitor Secretary of State Miguel de Vasconcelos, were to be found. The latter was killed on the spot and his body left to the wrath of the people who had suffered the foreign yoke for 60 years. The proud Duchess was ordered to leave the country, since the Duke of Bragança had been elected King of Portugal, as João IV.

A thrill of immense joy ran through the whole country, from North to South. Portugal was independent again.

SINCE THE RESTORATION

The unforgettable morning of December 1st was over, and Portugal was again master of its own destiny; but Spain was bound to react.

There was, for instance, the problem of the official recognition of João IV by the sovereigns of other States, particularly serious in the case of the Holy See, on acount of Spain's very great influence with the Papacy. But all difficulties were gradually removed thanks to the efficiency of politicians and the ability of military leaders.

The Dutch were thrown out of Brazil: in Africa, Angola was also taken back from them by Salvador Correia de Sá.

In the political sphere, the marriage of Catarina de Bragança, daughter of João IV, with Charles II of England was arranged, partly to counterbalance possible dangers arising from the Spanish-French peace treaty.

The old alliance of 1373 was strengthened, and by a formal treaty signed in 1661 England undertook to ensure the military defence of Portugal.

Years went by, and nothing of great moment took place.

Then came João V, our *Roi Soleil,* and his government gained enormous prestige, owing to the personality of the King himself and of the great statesmen who surrounded him.

The working and exploring of the gold mines in Brazil made it possible for the King to demonstrate lavishly Portugal's very great wealth. The Lisbon aqueduct was built, also the colossal Monastery at Mafra, the chapel of St. John the Baptist in the Church of São Roque in Lisbon, the Library of Coimbra University.

The navy also recovered its former power and importance, and thus it was able, together with the Venetian Fleet, to win the battle of Cape Matapan against the Turks, in 1716.This important victory resulted in a strengthening of the traditional ties with Rome (Pope Clement XI).

In the Museum of Royal Coaches, in Lisbon, there are a great many vehicles dating from this period, and among them three that took part in the magnificent Embassy to Pope Clement XI, the opulence of which caused the wonder of all Europe.

José I ascended the throne and appointed the Marquis of Pombal as his Prime Minister: a great statesman, but an implacable dictator also.

It is difficult to review in a few lines the life of this minister. If, on the one hand, he deserves our unreserved admiration for the economic development of the country in his time, for his energetic and enterprising spirit at the time of the great earthquake of 1755, and subsequent reconstruction of Lisbon, one cannot, on the other hand, lightly dismiss the persecution of many among the nobility who opposed him, or the means used finally to expel the Jesuits in 1760.

With the death of José I his daughter, Maria I, came to the throne. The victims of the Marquis demanded rehabilitation. Many got it, and the Marquis was banished from Lisbon to his estate.

Maria's reign was full of exemplary achievements. Surrounded by clever ministers she was able to start important reforms in various fields. In the meantime, in Europe, all religious and political accepted notions were shaken to their foundations and seem to crumble. In France, Louis XVI and Marie Antoinette were executed. Rousseau's ideals were hailed everywhere. Maria, highly concerned at these and other events, became insane. When she died her son João VI was the new King.

While still only the Regent, he had had to face the problem set by Napoleon — the ultimatum of 1807 — as part of the plan to destroy England. Napoleon and Charles IV had decided at Fontaine-bleau to divide Portugal between them. The Regent, foreseeing the invasion, transferred the Court and Government to Brazil, establishing the capital in Rio de Janeiro.

The invasion of Portugal was ordered. Junot, Soult, Masséna, in turn, commanded the waves that attempted to gain control of Portugal, but each wave was defeated after temporary success, by Portuguese resistance, with British help and under the command of Lord Wellington.

In 1811 the French retreat was final; Portugal had once more survived the crisis.

The new ideas, however, remained behind and were developing rapidly, not only in Portugal and Spain, but in Brazil and a few other South American States as well.

In Portugal things were not going well, and royal power was already very limited. Brazil proclaimed its independence in 1821.

Pedro became Emperor, as foreseen by his father João VI.

A few years later, a traditionalistic revolt broke out, under the leadership of young Prince Miguel, João's younger son, and after a victorious march on Lisbon, the King was invited to re-establish absolutism. For a time all was success, but later all was lost and Miguel was forced to go into exile, to Vienna.

With the death of João VI a serious problem arose, concerning the succession to the Throne. The liberal group chose Pedro of Brazil for their candidate, with the name of Pedro IV. Let us point out, however, that the latter had lost his right to inherit the Throne by becoming Emperor of Brazil.

In the meantime Miguel returned to Portugal and was enthusiastically acclaimed. Pedro finally renounced the Crown in Brazil and came to Portugal to defend the rights of his daughter, who would eventually be Maria II.

Miguel, aware that foreign powers were now aiding Maria's cause, finally gave up and went into exile, which was by then the only course open to him.

The Queen's husband, the German Prince Ferdinand of Saxe-Coburg, played an important part in defending and preserving monuments and art. From this time dates the Pena Castle at Sintra, which became the Royal summer residence.

With the death of Maria II, Pedro V came to the Throne, young and generous of heart. But he would die very soon, after having accomplished several reforms of great consequence. His brother Luís I, on the other hand, reigned for a long time, but witnessed the gradual twilight of royal power.

In 1889 Carlos I inherited the Crown, but Portuguese unity was greatly shaken. The previously prevailing state of chaos was made more serious still by England's incomprehensible attitude when in 1890 an ultimatum was sent to Portugal demanding the abandonment of certain territories connecting Angola and Mozambique.

Meanwhile, all the events were gradually working to the advantage of the enemies of the monarchy. Carlos I was murdered, together with his eldest son Prince Luís Filipe, on the 1st of February 1908. The younger son, Manuel, and his mother Queen Amélia de Orléans e Bragança, were saved. It was in the midst of tragic circumstances that the young King succeeded.

REPUBLIC

On 4th October 1910 a revolution broke out which put an end to the monarchy in Portugal. The next day the republican regime was proclaimed.

The first years were ones of great difficulties, aggravated by the effects of the 1st World War (1914-18), which brought about a terrible crisis all over Europe.

The Portuguese economy had already suffered harsh blows, and there was little left to do but accept the help of the League of Nations. This organisation was ready to aid us although it wanted to control our finances.

The proposed terms and conditions were unacceptable, but the problems could hardly be solved without taking severe economic measures.

On the grounds that the country was not ready for democracy in spite of the good intentions of some people, a revolution broke out on 28th May 1926 with the aim of setting up a strong government capable of solving the problems the country was facing.

As a consequence of the proposed objectives, Prof. Oliveira Salazar, who at that time held the chair of economics and finance at the University of Coimbra, was invited to become Minister of Finance.

Severe economic measures were decreed and little by little the finances of the country became sound once again.

In 1939, with the 2nd World War, new problems arose.

Thanks to her geographical position as the key to the Atlantic, Portugal was spared the devastation of war, although she naturally suffered the consequences of her neutrality.

Salazar, already Prime Minister and thanks to the authoritarian government which he dominated, came to direct the country's affairs by himself.

However, he did not manage to accompany the evolution of a New Europe based on participated government and a just and balanced social perspective.

After forty-three years of dictatorial government, Salazar died in 1970, leaving the country with serious social and political problems.

A colonial war that he sought to win by arms was doubtless a serious problem, one that was slowly but surely undermining Portuguese society.

He was succeeded as Prime Minister by Prof. Marcello Caetano, who was not able to control the situation.

The country's domestic problems were getting worse at a rate that worried everyone.

People were anxious for a change, in the hope that a balanced and just social programme would be decreed.

Since the problems were already beyond the control of the rulers themselves and discontent was growing in the Army due to the men it was losing in the African wars, a military movement broke out on 25th April 1974 and overthrew the government and restored the fundamental freedoms to the country.

The following year general elections were held. A new constitution was voted. In June 1976, General Ramalho Eanes was elected President of the Republic by universal suffrage.

Dr. Mário Soares, the leader of the party that received the most votes — the Socialist — was invited to form a Government, and promised to carry out a social project aimed at constructing a socialist society in freedom.

Portugal is thus continuing its destiny in a climate of confidence, based on the experience acquired in over eight centuries of history.

Photographs by the author

33 — Minho province is one of the gayest and most colourful of the country. At the festivities of Our Lady of the Agony, at Viana do Castelo, young women dress up in all the elegance of their richly decorated regional finery.

34 — Minho: Spinning flax.

35 — Viana do Castelo. A young Minho girl wearing one of the r
traditional dresses of Minho province.

36 — Soajo — Dramatic view of "Espigueiros" or "Canastros".

36 — Braga. S. Martinho da Gandra. Old house in granite.

37 — Lindoso. Serra do Soajo. A strange but real vision of a by-gone era. The old granite constructions "Espigueiros" are used to preserve the indian corn all the year round.

38 — Bragança.
38 — Guimarães. The castle here is considered to be the "cradle" of Portugal as an independent nation.

39 — Braga. The Good Jesus sanctuary.
40/41 — Minho. Working in the fields still maintains a charming oldfashioned look about it.

42 — Lamego. General panorama of the Lamego region seen from the belvedere of Pousada.

43 — Sandomil. (Beira Alta).

43 — Douro. The bustle of the grape harvest and wine-making.

44 — Douro. The grape harvest.

45 — Douro. These grapes will create the famous port wine.

46/47 — Oporto. The city is important enough to justify its pop
title of "Capital of the North"

48 — Oporto. View over the Douro, with the modern Arrábida bridge
in the background.

49.— Oporto. Avenida dos Aliados and the City Hal

50 — Aveiro. A seaweed-gathering boat.

50 — Aveiro.

51 — Palheiros de Mira. The daily toil.

52 — Curia. (Spa).

52 — Serra da Estrela.

53 — Tibães "Autumn". Park of the monaster

54 – Buçaco. The Hotel Palace, originally built for a royal residence.

55 – Buçaco. View of the dense woods surrounding the Palace Ho

56 — Figueira da Foz.

56 — Figueira da Foz. Regional pottery.

57 — Coimbra. The 12th-century Old Cathedral.

58/59 — Coimbra. The city and the Mondego river.

61 — Coimbra. The impressive university library, reflecting all the magnificence of the time of King João V.

62/63 — Conímbriga. Partial view of the Roman ruins.

60 — Coimbra. The famous university.

64 — Leiria. The city dominated by its fine mediaeval castle.

64 — São Pedro de Muel.

65 — Batalha. The Monastery of St. Mary of the Victory. Building
started under King João I in 1387.

66/67 — Batalha. General view of the Monastery.

68 — Batalha. The central nave of the Monastery.

69 — Batalha. The doorway to the Unfinished Chapels in the Monastery.

70 — Fátima. Cruz Alta.

71 — Fátima. Day of pilgrimage.

72/73 — Fátima. The candlelight processio

75 — Almourol. The Templar's castle.

4 — Fátima. An old pilgrim who had travelled many miles to be present.

75

77 — Tomar. The Tray Festival maintains an authentic mediaeval air.

80 — Nazaré. The fisherman's life.

81 — Nazaré. The "Washerwomen of Portugal".

89 – Alcobaça. The Monastery Church.

88 – Alcobaça. The Baroque front of the Cistercian Monastery of
Alcobaça, founded in the 12th century.

90 — Tomb of Inês de Castro (14th century).

90 — Tomb of King Pedro I (14th century).

91 – Óbidos. A mediaeval township which maintains intact all its
antique beauty.

92 — Óbidos. A street and the pillory.

92 — Mafra. The monastery founded by King João V in the 18th century.

93 — Torres Vedras. A typical windmill of the region.

94/95 — Lisbon. The Alfama quarter and the Tagus.

96 — Lisbon. The Historical
Art Museum and Gallery.
The Prince's Panel, from
the polyptych attributed to
Nuno Gonçalves. (Close of
the 15th century).

97 — Lisbon. The Historical
Art Museum and Gallery.
The Belém Monstrance, a
masterpiece of Portuguese
craftsmanship in gold
(16th century).

98/99 — Lisbon. The Jeró-
nimos Monastery, built by
King Manuel I (the Ma-
nueline style — 16th
century).

100/101 — Lisbon. The
Belém Tower, a 16th
century fortress built in the
Manueline style.

102 — Lisbon. View of the Edward VII Park, with flowering jacarandas.

102 — Lisbon. The Rossio or King Pedro IV Square (he was the first Emperor of Brazil).

103 — Lisbon. The Tagus Bridge.

103 — Lisbon. The National Coach Museum is one of the major attractions for visitors to the city.

104/105 — Lisbon. Praça do Comércio (or Black Horse Square), built after the 1755 earthquake.

106/107 — Lisbon. The Cool Greenhouses.

108/109 — Queluz. Queluz Palace was built in the 18th century for a royal summer residence.

110/111 — Queluz. The Royal Palace. This is the Don Quixote Room, where Pedro I, the first Emperor of Brazil, was born and died.

112/113 — Sintra. Town Palace. It served, from the 14th century on, as a royal residence.
114/115 — Sintra. The Town Palace. The Hall of Escutcheons.
116/117 — Sintra. The Town Palace. The Hall of Swans.

118/119 — Sintra. The Pena Palace, built in 1840 on the site of a 16th century monastery.

120/121 — Sintra. The Pena Palace. Chapel' of the former Monastery (16th century).
122/123 — Cascais. View of the bay.

124 — Cascais. The catch is landed.

124 -- Cascais. A pleasant corner in this important tourist resort.

125 — Cascais. Palace of the Earls of Castro Guimarães, now a museum.

126 — Estoril. The Garden and Casino.

126 — Estoril. Tamariz beach.

127 — Estoril. The bay by night.

127 — Estoril. View of the town centre.

128/129 — Estoril. The casino at night.

130 — Santarém. The capital of Ribatejo province, famous for the breeding of bulls for the ring. The herdsmen demonstrate their fantastic skill and dexterity at the International Ribatejo Fair.

131 — Bull-catching. A group of bold lads take hold of the bull and only let go when the bull is quite overpowered.

30 — Bullfighting on horseback in the old-fashioned Portuguese style.

132 — Prickly-pear bushes.

133 — Sesimbra. The fish auction begins.

133 — Sesimbra. Fishing harbour.

134 — Monsarás. Menhir.

134 — Sines. The fishing harbour.

135 — View of Alentejo province. The cork-oak is important to the Portuguese economy, for Portugal produces close on half of the world's cork.

136 — Évora. The Moura gateway.

136 — Évora. View of the "museum-city", with the old Romanic cathedral looming in the background.

137 — Évora. The imposing columns of the Roman temple dedicated to Diana (second century A.D.).

138 — Castelo de Vide. Chapel of N. S. da Penha.

139 — Beja. The Keep of the mediaeval castle

138 — Castelo de Vide. The town fountain.

140 — Sagres. Cape St. Vincent, at the south-western corner of Portugal, is closely linked with the work of Prince Henry the Navigator and the vast enterprise of the Discoveries.

140 — Sagres. The Atlantic coast.

141 — Lagos. Monument to Prince Henry. The stones of the paving are so placed as to recall the waves of the sea, so constant an element in our national history, and even more so during the Age of the Discoveries.

142/143 — Lagos. There are beautiful caves along the coast from Don'Ana beach to Piedade Point.

144/145 — Portimão. One of the most important fishing harbours in the country. In the background the buildings and big hotels of the cosmopolitan Praia da Rocha seaside resort.

146 — Portimão. Fishing-boats.

147 — Praia da Rocha: detail of the Algarve coast

148/149 — Praia da Rocha. The ideal seaside resort, all year round, thanks to its climatic features.

150 — Algarve. The typical chimneys are part of the decorative landscape.

151 — Algarve. Almond blossom.

152/153 — Algarve. Thousands of blossoming almond-trees, in late January, cover the province in beauty.

154 — Praia da Don'Ana.

154 — Tavira. Salt-pans.

155 — Algarve. Mimosa blossom (January

156/157 — Albufeira. View over the town and its busy fishing harbour.
This is one of the most popular Algarve resorts for young
people.

158/159 — Vilamoura. Houses in the Algarve which, though modern, stil maintain the charming stylisnness of the region.

160 — Vilamoura. Algarve sunset.